South Carolina

By Janelle Cherrington

Consultant
Nanci R. Vargus, Ed.D.
Assistant Professor of Literacy
University of Indianapolis, Indianapolis, Indiana

Children's Press®
A Division of Scholastic Inc.
New York Toronto London Auckland Sydney
Mexico City New Delhi Hong Kong
Danbury, Connecticut

Designer: Herman Adler Design
Photo Researcher: Caroline Anderson
The photo on the cover shows Boone Hall Plantation, Charleston.

Library of Congress Cataloging-in-Publication Data

Cherrington, Janelle.
  South Carolina / by Janelle Cherrington.
     p. cm. – (Rookie read–about geography)
Summary: A simple introduction to South Carolina, focusing on its
regions and their geographical features.
Includes index.
  ISBN 0-516-22743-2 (lib. bdg.)   0-516-27329-9 (pbk.)
  1. South Carolina–Juvenile literature. 2. South
Carolina–Geography–Juvenile literature. [1. South Carolina.] I.
Title. II. Series.
  F269.3.C48 2003
  975.7–dc21

                                        2003000464

CHILDREN'S PRESS, and ROOKIE READ-ABOUT®,
and associated logos are trademarks and or registered trademarks
of Scholastic Library Publishing. SCHOLASTIC and associated logos
are trademarks and or registered trademarks of Scholastic Inc.

1 2 3 4 5 6 7 8 9 10 R 12 11 10 09 08 07 06 05 04 03

Do you know which state
is shaped like a triangle?

It is the state of South Carolina!

Can you find South Carolina on this map? It is located in the southeastern part of the United States.

CANADA

WASHINGTON
OREGON
IDAHO
MONTANA
NORTH DAKOTA
SOUTH DAKOTA
WYOMING
NEBRASKA
IOWA
MINNESOTA
WISCONSIN
MICHIGAN
NEW HAMPSHIRE
VERMONT
MAINE
NEW YORK
MASSACHUSETTS
RHODE ISLAND
CONNECTICUT
NEW JERSEY
DELAWARE
MARYLAND
Washington, D.C.
PENNSYLVANIA
OHIO
NEVADA
UTAH
CALIFORNIA
COLORADO
KANSAS
MISSOURI
ILLINOIS
INDIANA
KENTUCKY
WEST VIRGINIA
VIRGINIA
ARIZONA
NEW MEXICO
OKLAHOMA
ARKANSAS
TENNESSEE
NORTH CAROLINA
SOUTH CAROLINA
TEXAS
LOUISIANA
MISSISSIPPI
ALABAMA
GEORGIA
FLORIDA

ALASKA
CANADA
MEXICO
HAWAII

North
West
East
South

5

South Carolina has three major parts, or regions (REE-juhnz). The biggest part is the Coastal Plain. Some people call it the "low country."

Beach

Swamp

On the Coastal Plain
there are beaches, swamps,
farmland, and forests.

The Sea Islands are part
of the Coastal Plain.
They are off the coast
of South Carolina.

Many people visit these
islands every year. They
come to golf, fish, swim,
and rest.

Pelican

Birds visit the Sea Islands, too. Many birds stop on the islands when they fly south for the winter and north for the summer.

The Grand Strand is part
of the Coastal Plain, too.
Strand means "shore,"
or "beach."

The Grand Strand is 60
miles long. Many people
like to swim and play golf
on the Grand Strand.

NORTH CAROLINA

North
West · East
South

SOUTH
CAROLINA

Myrtle
Beach ·

Grand Strand

GEORGIA

SCALE 1 inch = 50 miles

0   Miles   50

0   Kilometers   80

ATLANTIC
OCEAN

13

14

Myrtle Beach is the largest town on the Strand. Thousands of tourists go there each year.

The two biggest cities in South Carolina are on the Coastal Plain.

Columbia is the state's largest city. It is also the capital. Columbia is located in the middle of the state.

Capitol Building

18

Many people have government (GUHV-urn-muhnt) jobs. Other people make cloth in factories.

Some people work in banks and hospitals.

Charleston is South
Carolina's second largest
city. It is 100 years older
than the United States
of America.

Charleston has many
beautiful old buildings.

21

South Carolina has lots of small towns, too. Almost half the people in the state live in small towns.

Other people live in the country.

South Carolina's second region is called the Piedmont (PEED-mahnt). Some people call it part of the "up country."

The Piedmont has many
companies. They make
computers, car parts,
and furniture.

There are many farms in the Piedmont. Some of these farms grow more peaches than any other state, except California.

The Carolina wren is the state bird. It likes to nest in farm buildings.

The Blue Ridge is the third and smallest region of the state.

It has a lot of waterfalls, streams, lakes, and mountain trails.

Which part of South Carolina do you like best?

29

Words You Know

Carolina wren

Charleston

Columbia

military

Myrtle Beach

peaches

swamp

triangle

Index

About the Author

Janelle Cherrington has written more than 50 books for children of all ages. She works in New York City, where she lives with her husband and her cat. South Carolina is one of her favorite places to visit.

Photo Credits

Photographs © 2003: Photo Researchers, NY: 3, 31 bottom right (David M. Grossman), 25 (Will & Deni McIntyre); Photri Inc.: 17, 30 bottom left (Bill Barley), 21, 30 top right (Arnold John Kaplan), 7, 31 bottom left (William Kulik); Stock Boston/Jerry Howard: 26, 31 top right; Superstock, Inc.: cover; Transparencies Inc.: 14, 31 top left (Cheryl Callaman), 18, 30 bottom right (Robert Clark), 6, 9, 10, 22, 29 (Jane Faircloth); Visuals Unlimited/William J. Weber: 27, 30 top left.

Maps by Bob Italiano